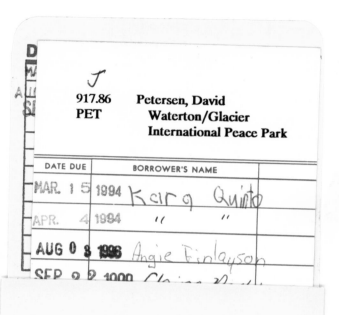

A New True Book

WATERTON-GLACIER

INTERNATIONAL
PEACE PARK

By David Petersen

CHILDRENS PRESS®
CHICAGO

A waterfall in Waterton
Lakes National Park

Project Editor: Fran Dyra
Design: Margrit Fiddle

Library of Congress Cataloging-in-Publication Data

Petersen, David.
    Waterton-Glacier International Peace Park / by
David Petersen.
        p.   cm. — (A New true book)
    Includes index.
    Summary: Depicts the wildlife, mountains, glaciers,
wildflowers, and other sights protected by the
Waterton-Glacier Park, an international park created in
1932 by the Canadian and American governments.
    ISBN 0-516-01946-5
    1. Glacier National Park (Mont.)—Juvenile
literature. 2. Waterton Lakes National Park (Alta.)—
Juvenile literature. [1. Glacier National Park (Mont.)
2. Waterton Lakes National Park (Alta.)
3. National parks and reserves.] I. Title.
F737.G5P48 1992
917.86'52—dc20   92-9208
                                              CIP
                                               AC

PHOTO CREDITS

© Cameramann International, Inc.—16 (left), 20, 22, 24

Glacier National Park—11

H. Armstrong Roberts—© T. Algire, 7 (bottom); © T. Ulrich, 7 (center), 38; © M. Schneiders, 8 (top); © R. Lamb, 12; © Ed Cooper, 36; © L. Burton, 44

© Jerry Hennen—21 (right), 27

Odyssey/Chicago—© Kevin O. Mooney, 8 (bottom); © E. S. Curtis, 42 (2 photos)

Photri—© MacDonald Photography, 34

© Branson Reynolds—16 (right), 25, 26, 41 (right)

© Chris Roberts—43

Root Resources—© Alan G. Nelson, Cover; © John Kohout, 13 (right); © Clarence Postmus, 14

© James P. Rowan—33

© Bob and Ira Spring—29, 30

Tom Stack & Associates—© Joe McDonald, 21 (left); © Mark Newman, 39

TSW-CLICK/Chicago—© Tom Dietrich, 15 (top)

Valan—© S. J. Krasemann, 2, 5; © Dennis Schmidt, 4; © M. G. Kingshott, 7 (top); © Pam E. Hickman, 13 (left); © Hälle Flygare, 15 (bottom); © J.R. Page, 19 (right); © Jeannie R. Kemp, 31; © Harold V. Green, 32, 45; © Murray O'Neill, 35; © John Fowler, 41 (left)

Horizon Graphics—10

Tom Dunnington—18, 19 (right)

Cover—Waterton-Glacier National Peace Park

TABLE OF CONTENTS

Grizzly bears grow up to 8 feet (2.4 meters) long and weigh about 400 pounds (182 kilograms). Grizzly bears once lived throughout the Rocky Mountains. But so many have been killed by hunters that they are now threatened.

GRIZZLIES AND GLACIERS

From a mountaintop, a photographer spotted a huge grizzly bear splashing in a beaver pond. As he watched, the big brown bear climbed out of the water and shook itself like a big dog.

That photographer was very lucky. Most people never get to see a grizzly bear.

Today only a few hundred grizzly bears live south of the Canadian border. And their survival is threatened. Not enough wilderness is left to support many animals as big and wild as grizzlies.

One of the few places where grizzly bears and gray wolves still roam free is Glacier National Park in Montana.

Next to Glacier, across the border in Alberta, Canada, there is another wonderful park. It's called Waterton Lakes National Park.

Red Rock Canyon (above) in Waterton Lakes Park. The gray wolf (right) has recently returned to the park. The "Hanging Gardens" (below) are in the Logan Pass area of Glacier Park.

Swiftcurrent Lake and Mount Wilbur (above) in Glacier National Park.
Forests of pine and fir trees (below) cover much of the park area.

A PARK FOR PEACE

In 1895, the Canadian government created Waterton Lakes Park. They wanted to protect the area's wildlife and its natural beauty. In 1910, the United States Congress created Glacier National Park for the same reasons.

People soon realized that the two parks belonged together. They had the same ecosystem. They shared the same rivers and lakes and

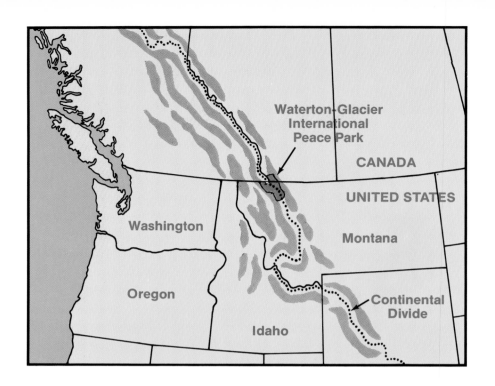

had the same kinds of plants and animals.

Everything in an ecosystem is connected. Each part depends on all the other parts for its welfare.

Since the two parks were already joined by nature,

Canada and the United States decided to make the parks a symbol of the peace and friendship between the two nations.

Thus, in 1932, Waterton-Glacier International Peace Park became the world's first

The dedication of Waterton-Glacier International Peace Park took place on June 18, 1932.

A glacial lake at the foot of Mount Gould in Glacier National Park

international park. It covers an area of 1.4 million acres (566,560 hectares) and includes some of the most magnificent scenery in the world.

In Waterton-Glacier,

The McDonald Creek flows through Glacier National Park. Narada Falls (inset) is one of the many beautiful waterfalls found in the park.

mountains like giant horns pierce the clouds. There are high mountain valleys where the snow never melts. There are sparkling blue lakes and rivers, and waterfalls by the hundreds.

13

The American bald eagle is protected by federal laws in the United States.

About sixty species of wild animals live in the park. And nearly 200 species of birds, including America's national symbol, the bald eagle, are found in Waterton-Glacier. In addition, more than a thousand species of plants, many of them wildflowers, cover its meadows.

Beargrass blooms along a creek in Glacier National Park. The beautiful blue camas lily (inset) has a delicious bulb that was used as a food source by Native Americans in the Rocky Mountains. But one kind of bulb, called the "death camas," is poisonous.

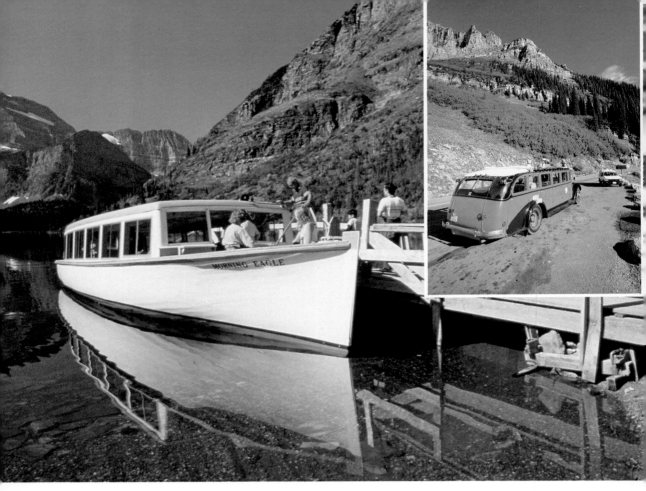

Visitors to the park can take boat trips on the lakes. Tour buses (inset) take people to see the magnificent scenery of the park.

The park offers ranger-guided nature walks and campfire programs as well as tours by bus, boat, and horseback.

HOW DID IT COME TO BE?

The steep Rocky Mountains and snow-packed valleys of Waterton-Glacier were made by natural forces.

A billion years ago, these mountains and valleys did not exist. Instead, the land was flat and covered much of the time by a shallow sea.

Every year, tons of sediments, such as mud and sand, were washed into the water. Eventually, they

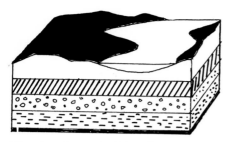

The land started to change over one billion years ago. Sediments washed into an ancient sea. When the water dried up, the sediment hardened into stone. As the waters came and went, the layers of sediment and stone grew and grew.

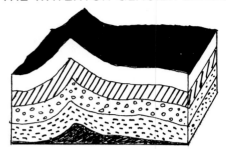

About 75 million years ago, a section of the Earth's crust buckled up.

settled to the bottom and piled up.

Each time the water dried up, the sediments hardened into stone. Then the water returned and another layer of sediments was deposited.

Over millions of years, hundreds of layers of sedimentary rock were formed in this way. Then, about 75 million years ago, a

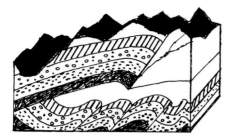

In some places, one section of the Earth's crust slid over another section.

The layers of sedimentary rock can be seen in this formation at Waterton Lakes Park.

great upheaval deep within the Earth caused the flat land to buckle.

In some places, the ground actually cracked open and one side of the crack pushed up over the other. In this way, the Rocky Mountains of Waterton-Glacier were formed.

Tilted layers of rock clearly show where the Earth buckled up and was broken.

Today, we see the ancient layers of sedimentary rocks as lines, or "steps," on the mountainsides. The layers are tilted and uneven where the Earth was buckled up and broken.

After the mountains were

A waterfall (left) rushes down a steep, rocky mountainside. Grinnell Glacier (right) is covered with glacial debris.

formed, streams of rain and melting snow rushed down their slopes. Over time, the rushing water cut V-shaped gullies in the mountainsides.

Finally, about a million years ago, the first glaciers appeared.

Jackson Glacier lies high in a mountain valley.

THE ICE AGE

A glacier is a huge mass
of moving ice. For thousands
of years during the Ice Age,

North America grew colder

and colder. It was like a winter that never ended.

Every year the snow piled deeper and deeper. Under its own increasing weight, the snow was slowly compressed into ice. These masses of ice were hundreds of feet thick.

When gravity began to pull the ice masses down the valleys, they became glaciers. As the ice in Waterton-Glacier moved slowly down the steep gullies, it scraped against their rocky walls.

Looking into the McDonald Valley from Going-to-the-Sun Road

Thousands of years of this grinding action carved the narrow, V-shaped gullies into the wide, U-shaped valleys we see at the park, today.

Sometimes, two glaciers grinding on opposite sides of the same mountain or ridge

formed an arête. An

arête is a tall, thin, jagged ridge. The most famous arête in Glacier National Park is along the Continental Divide. It is called the Garden Wall.

When three glaciers ground away at the same

The "Garden Wall" is a famous arête near Logan Pass.

Reynolds Mountain as seen from Logan Pass

mountain from three different sides, a horn was formed. These horns look like giant, three-sided pyramids. Reynolds Mountain at Waterton-Glacier is a famous horn.

26

Then, about 12,000 years ago, the glaciers began to melt. They left behind huge piles of dirt, stones, and other debris that had been swept up by the moving ice. These giant piles of glacial debris are called moraines.

A moraine has dirt, stones, and other debris deposited by a glacier.

When a moraine was deposited across a stream, it acted as a natural dam. And behind each of these glacial dams, a lake was formed. Most of Waterton-Glacier's lakes formed in this way.

Today, there are about fifty glaciers in the park. However, these glaciers are relatively small and "young." They are not related to the ancient giants that carved the landscape long ago.

A glacier's movement often causes crevasses–

A ranger guides hikers past a crevasse on Grinnell Glacier.

deep cracks in the ice. These crevasses make glaciers dangerous to walk on. But if you are led by a park ranger, you can hike across the glaciers safely.

29

Hikers on the trail to Grinnell Glacier

TOURING THE PARK

Waterton-Glacier International Peace Park has hundreds of miles of hiking trails. Step onto any one of them, and soon you'll be in true wilderness.

Waterton Lake camping area

Some trails lead to hidden lakes where cutthroat trout swim and jump.

Some trails lead to remote campsites. Other trails lead up into the mountains, where you can look down upon a forest of living green.

Visitors can tour the park on horseback.

If you'd rather ride than walk, you can rent a horse. And if you like water, you can take a boat tour on several of the larger lakes.

However, most visitors see the park from their cars.

Waterton-Glacier has many scenic roads, but the most exciting road is the Going-to-the-Sun Road. This 52-mile (83–kilometer) journey on Going-to-the-Sun Road takes you from the west side of the mountains and Lake

Going-to-the-Sun Road runs along a mountainside.

St. Mary Lake as seen from Sun Point

McDonald, to the east side
and the St. Mary Lake.

Logan Pass is the highest
point on Going-to-the-Sun
Road. It is 6,680 feet (2,036
meters) above sea level.

Sharp, rocky ridges and blue glacial lakes
are typical of the scenery in the park.

Up there, all the snow
never completely melts. It is
a perfect place for mountain
goats.

These amazing animals
are white, with long, shaggy

35

The amazing mountain goat is right at home
on the steepest mountainsides.

hair. They need their heavy coats because they stay up in the mountains all winter. Mountain goats are the world's best climbers.

Sometimes, mountain goats let you get close to them. But remember that smart people enjoy wildlife from a safe distance.

Mountain goats are wild animals with long, sharp horns. When frightened or angry, any wild animal can be dangerous.

A gray wolf feeding on a moose. Predators help maintain a balance in nature, keeping the herds of prey animals from becoming too large for their food supply.

OTHER WILDLIFE

Another interesting animal in Waterton-Glacier Park is the gray wolf. Wolves are carnivores—they eat only meat. And they get their meat by hunting. Animals

that hunt other animals for
food are called predators.
   Most of the wolves, grizzly
bears, mountain lions,
and other predators that
once roamed North
America have been killed off,
because people used to

A mother grizzly bear with her cub. Mother bears are
very dangerous and unpredictable when protecting their young.

think predators were bad. The wolf, like the grizzly, is now an endangered species in the United States.

For a long time, there were no wolves in Glacier National Park. Then, in the early 1980s, a pack of wolves moved south from Canada into Glacier National Park. The members of this "Magic Pack" were the first wolves seen in Glacier in fifty years.

Today, the descendants of the Magic Pack make up two groups called the North and

Many wild animals, including the bighorn sheep (left) and the tiny pika (above), are found in Waterton-Glacier International Peace Park.

South Camas Pack. The wolves of the Camas Pack live in the northwestern part of the park.

Today, Glacier National Park is one of the few places south of Canada where it is still possible to see both grizzlies and wolves.

41

Flathead mother (left)
carries her baby in a traditional
cradleboard. A Piegan
family (above) inside their lodge.

WATERTON-GLACIER'S NATIVE HERITAGE

By the time the first
European explorers
wandered into Glacier
country, Native Americans
had been visiting the area

for thousands of years. Some tribes that have always lived in the Glacier area are the Blackfeet, Bloods, Piegans, Stoneys, and Flatheads. Many of the natural features of Waterton-Glacier are named for them.

Blackfeet elders gather at Browning, Montana.

St. Mary Lake and Sun Mountain

THE CROWN OF THE CONTINENT

Flat-topped Chief Mountain stands alone in Glacier National Park.

The snow-capped mountains, the massive glaciers, the fascinating wildlife, and the beautiful wildflowers are all there for you to see.

When you do, you'll understand why Waterton-Glacier International Peace Park is called the Crown of the Continent.

45

WORDS YOU SHOULD KNOW

arête (ah • RET) — a thin, knifelike mountain ridge carved by two glaciers grinding on opposite sides of a mountain

carnivore (KAR • nih • vohr) — an animal that eats only meat

compressed (kum • PREST) — pressed together by a great force or weight

crevasse (krih • VASS) — a deep crack in the ice of a glacier

debris (deh • BREE) — broken and scattered fragments of rocks

deposit (dih • PAH • zit) — to drop or lay down

descendant (dih • SEN • dint) — a child or a grandchild; a person or animal that comes later in a family line

ecosystem (EK • oh • sis • tem) — an area that shares the same kinds of places and the same kinds of animal and plant life

endangered (en • DAYN • jerd) — in danger of dying out

explorer (ex • PLOR • er) — a person who travels to far-off places to learn about the land and the people there

glacier (GLAY • sher) — a thick mass of ice that moves slowly across land or down a mountain

gravity (GRAV • ih • tee) — the force that pulls things toward the Earth

moraines (mor • AINZ) — hills and ridges made of gravel, rocks, and sand deposited by a glacier

predator (PREH • duh • ter) — an animal that kills and eats other animals

sedimentary rock (sed • ih • MEN • tree RAHK) — rock that forms when a body of water dries up and the layers of sediments on the bottom harden into stone

sediments (SED • ih • ments) — small particles, such as mud and sand, deposited on the bottom of a body of water

symbol (SIM • bil) — a thing that stands for something else

wilderness (WIL • der • ness) — a region not inhabited by people

wildlife (WYLD • lyfe) — living things that are found in the wild; animals that are not raised by people

INDEX

About the Author

David Petersen teaches writing at Fort Lewis College in Durango, Colorado. A self-described "older child," he has been exploring and enjoying the Grand Canyon for more than forty years.